NOVA

THE NATIONAL POETRY SERIES

The National Poetry Series was established in 1978 to ensure the publication of five poetry books annually through participating publishers. Publication is funded by the late James A. Michener, The Copernicus Society of America, Edward J. Piszek, the Lannan Foundation, and the National Endowment for the Arts.

1999 Competition Winners

Tenaya Darlington (Wisconsin), *Madame Deluxe*
SELECTED BY LAWSON INADA
PUBLISHED BY COFFEE HOUSE PRESS

Eugene Gloria (Massachusetts), *Drivers at the Short-Time Motel*
SELECTED BY YUSEF KOMUNYAKAA
PUBLISHED BY VIKING PENGUIN

Corey Marks (Texas), *Renunciation*
SELECTED BY PHILIP LEVINE
PUBLISHED BY UNIVERSITY OF ILLINOIS PRESS

Dionisio Martinez (Florida), *Climbing Back*
SELECTED BY JORIE GRAHAM
PUBLISHED BY W. W. NORTON

Standard Schaefer (California), *Nova*
SELECTED BY NICK PIOMBINO
PUBLISHED BY SUN & MOON PRESS

N O V A

Standard Schaefer

NEW AMERICAN POETRY SERIES: 36

☀ & ☾ PRESS

LOS ANGELES · 2001

Sun & Moon Press
A Program of The Contemporary Arts Educational Project, Inc.
a nonprofit corporation
6026 Wilshire Boulevard, Los Angeles, California 90036
www.sunmoon.com

This edition first published in 2001 by Sun & Moon Press
10 9 8 7 6 5 4 3 2 1
FIRST EDITION

Excerpts from some form of this manuscript have appeared in
*Ribot, New American Poetry, Fence, Combo, Rampike, Syllogism, Misc. Proj.,
Columbia Review, Lyric&, TinFish, Lowghost, Syntactics* and *Volt*.
The author would like to thank the editors of these magazines.

Cover: *Moving Out [Star Field II]*, by Vija Celmins
Design: Katie Messborn
Typography: Guy Bennett

LIBRARY OF CONGRESS CATALOGING IN PUBLICATION DATA
Schaefer, Standard [1971]
Nova
p. cm ƒ (New American Poetry Series: 36)
ISBN: 1-55713-404-9
I. Title. II. Series.
811'.54ƒdc20

Printed in the United States of America on acid-free paper.

In memory of FLORA MAE LEE

ACKNOWLEDGMENTS

These people helped guide this manuscript through revision: Martha Ronk, Cathy Wagner, Leslie Scalapino, Jacques Debrot, and Emily Grossman. Their encouragement and advice are greatly appreciated.

VLADMIR: We have kept our appointment and that's an
          end to that. We aren't saints, but at least we kept
          our appointment. How many people can boast as
          much?
ESTRAGON: Billions.

—SAMUEL BECKETT

FORT

LUSTER

malaria: bad air
brown wave after brown wave
branching at the start, the glance
scratched for a glance at the scratch
of ants, ends or something to burn
but after the games of chance, chance
and a change of sides, severed only by daylight
and restored to the littoral where clarity
is vitiated by clarity

MANOS

the conditions: brown ankle, brown river,
dust specks drifting in the last of the light
the middle moving lower, forward
theirs to have and theirs to keep, the distance
banks in the distance, eels along the highway
and series of tolls
the hand that cannot stay
the distance

RIO

set to taste the dust brought to the mouth
the earth led from drunkeness
levanto mi copa pero llega nunca el dia
but these fumbling hands against *la velocidad*
and the luster *pero no quiero ver, no importa nadie*
la velocidad que no llega nunca
stabbed by daylight and fumbling through the hands
a splintered river

GALVESTON

recited the Lord's prayer and was hired
to the town to take the pledge
to the honky tonk to take exception
in the morning to the fort with the teenage accountants,
with a surplus of munitions
hidden along the sea wall between the tall grass and cattails,
a whiff of brig, a swig of sleep
then bent again like the numbers amid tall hats and coattails
comes awake in the arms of a slot machine
but in the evening, smudged ledgers
and in the morning hedging the machinations
sometimes plagiarism, sometimes smarts
but almost always worth millions in parts

BATTLESHIP

zeroes end to end or stacked backwards
a million through mettle, then another through crude
scrappy as a millionaire in the future
and set out like hooks to trap the prom queen
who goes south for scraps of metal
accepts the first offer, picks up on the first ring
but the teenage accountant had become surrounded
asphalt beneath the tires and a hollow, whining scream
packaged static and built a business out of hurricanes
despite that one hair left behind on a pillow
or a widow turning up in the brine

RED HEADED STRANGER

High as a derrick, and sometimes despised,
the long thigh—more beautiful than a stolen horse,
but behaving about as well and shallow as a heiress in the
          middle of a mood
but to hell with love as a dying ember or her face in a well
well, don't mind if I do, don't mind at all,
hope that'll do ya, but always remember, I don't mind

CONCEPTION

Alpha, Bravo, Charlie...
a twitch in the leg, a witch at the helm
whether at a petting party or a poker game
greeted all her guest in her pajamas
but "white, aimless signals" leveled all thought
like a stack of documents changing hands
or a banana passed between cabana boys
then tossed like towels into international waters, the cork
caught in the throat, but not a thing to complain about,
just a rodeo inside her, where for him Korea remained

AUGUST 21, 1971

Sierra, Tango, Alpha, November
ten pounds inspiration, one inch discipline
I'm a medium but the future looks hollow
around the edges, evaporation
the light shallow and the smell of balloons
the air of inflation won't make no mind,
don't mind at all if it smells like home-cooking and turns
          out a river,
each day, progressively more sawed-off

13

FIDDLE

hills under blankets, then heels in the ice house
crawled out of a barrel to find a riffle instead of a spine
ankles and elbows in constant contemplation
      smoke through the radio smeared into velvet
delivered to the ribs and easily recited
like actual symbols for artificial facts
like a shadow in a doorway like his father's back
but it was only a guess in his pajamas or an hour along the shore
bouncing in a lap before pulling up a stool, and staring at the
      grate in the floor

PINE

there is a justice beyond judgment, just past the trees,
just us and these endless pines, tougher than barbed wire
or the talk of rights while the rice is served —
a self-made meal — ice and scotch stirred in a sliding glass
the crash of the window as he put his fist through.
the fist darkening the page, the first withdrawn
as if reaching for the salt, but the salt wandering down from his
      eyes, as he reached up for the roll of fifties and hundreds
kept in the glove box with the golf balls and pajamas,
but how many shows till he shows
how many times he falls through that mirror
the warm rear of the bird when reaching for the egg or lifting
      the limbs
the luster of the universe coming loose in the use and pulse of
      language, but who can sleep with wind off the concrete
las estrellas apagadas por el huracán.
the eye wandering aimlessly, indefatigably through the pines,
      back and forth, sliding the glass, to the trees — to be crazy
      again.

CYCLONE

It was a gusty kind of house, rambling, brick on the inside
and on the outside the fence was all white
like the jury, only more aimless. South and west, abstract
as a wall casually tossed up, but invisible as the hand that fed us.
I gave them mine and they gave me theirs, and we waltzed in
     front of
the headlights, outbound like rabbits or leaded gas,
the constant sleet of golf balls bearing down and wild engines,
sirens on the CB — and the old man's habit of high beams
cuando no pueden dormir en la noche, todos no pueden dormir
wind off the concrete *pero no hay paz entre nosotros*
having blown past the horrible immensity of no sirens singing,
     no crow where no sigh subjective
when the question is posed in relations of force.

BOARDER

A warm and gutsy breeze in the room next door
and a lively bounce on a knee
where Aunts are obvious.

Taught bible school to millionaires and Latin to parakeets,
     sometimes Spanish
But always dismantled relations of reference
with a wedge of pie, lump of sugar or a caress
until the pancreas grew as obvious and as yellow
as the rose of Texas down some fairway built on breezes.
Down with all of it, my dear Sweet Clump of Roses,
Down with ants, worms, and lumpy fairways
where school teachers go to live like millionaires.

SPOKES

From the pieces, pieces,
Spinning between "and" and "again"
the river, the fence then chorizo, egg and a nap
spoke only Spanish when spoken to
but it didn't mean a thing
when wet and trundling beneath satellites power lines, west
toward a Paris to come
as any boy from Texas would *cuando pienso en un pino*—
such vast properties: salt, shale, *la distancia y la velocidad*
followed them toward the source of dimples on a golf ball
in the wind through the pines, the pining to go to bed
and the ants that sleep there.

OCCIDENTAL

Freon at last, but
"I don't have the television myse'f. Relations do."
"We do likes it often, but only a little at a time,"
preferring a slow and tender swig to the syllabus
which was Sally followed by Becky,
do something free or at least break things
but really only *chistes para desorientar la policía*
allegiance to the agenda, but "just doing my job"
pretty sure it was the same for Revere,
said the occupant who was *absente* whenever possible
knew full well there was no outside of the test
strictly an older knowledge as in *veritas simplex oratio est*
but blinded by some flash of new color,
with one black pebble on the calendar
but onward through college and oncology
learning insects and intellect only sound alike

made a list to eliminate the country and city of your birth,
the paint peeling away of what was left of Becky waving from the
      flowers,
too red to be a cup of light, too stale to be a cut above
although both described her lips whether whistling or reciting
her Latin: *otium cum dignitate*, said the girl
who liked Coast soap and counting
to three, and snapping her fingers:
"No leisure without dignity."

LA CIUDAD DE LOS ANGELES

X-ray, Yankee, Zulu. Off with this redneck Ju Ju.
Wear bolder, roll up your windows, and sleep it off,
said *el conquistador* to the occupant who never stopped asking,
      "What fort?"
and took the palm beneath the palms to that city
that was never mysterious only exclusive
everyone's crying "Where is the heart?"
habría hecho algo diferente—no es distinto
"My heart is a foreign object,"
the terrible ambiguity, the unproven click
of a latch swung in both directions

DIXI

Urine of white wolf, feather of crow
place in an old hat at the center of a circle,
rub the fish eye with blood of bat, stirring
the fatigue; it is only music. Listen for it
between fugue states and friends in another bar
of Dixie, another glass of hope

that work will conquer all,
labor omnia vincit
before the lord's prayer recited backward
sive margaritas ante porcos
the harp bleats the dead have lost all confidence
but in a pinch, use the words
mox nox in rem or *mutum in parvo*
learn to fiddle less, tickle few minikens
be they brides or just a walk in the brine
and under no circumstance mention Dixie to Trixie
flaunt not the rose even *post festum venisti*
now that the truth is out and our daily bread is in
There's a new south rising against the sliding glass
of a dead language
come to settle a strictly older score between the *entre nos* and
        the intra nos,
where *otium cum dignitate et mox nox in rem*
and when early to the autopsy be not ashamed
it's never too soon or certain to begin

OVALNESS

After an evening spent splitting quarks to quills, one solitary oval grew weary and slipped his fingers between the covers of a crude and common book—the sort offered to children—when he was accosted by some new vapor creeping out a grogshop he once had known, some feast days past, during the Paper Stages of superstitions not even the patrons would tolerate, least of all the sort mimped here:

"No more remorse about this shape you're in or the indifference to," beseeched a musty little orb, "A circle must not be allowed to lament its having been penned flimsier than a sphere."

But drowsy from this midnight calling and lacking any appeal to law, the oval tapped twice his foot in dispute and volleyed a tepid retort:

"The adders are out again tonight, do they slither after a missing wink and slur the same routine? I deplore your loops of consciousness, clocks. Why must all your arguments bubble insufficiently toward perfection, where there are no pages to bring a page, only this long division too much between us ambitiously expressed in One Impeachable Substance, with no sky no grass and yet all things are, 'as it were,' as all things have always been—a matter little less than 'if'—for God was not built in a bottle, neither in time nor distance…distance… time…all the Occupant lets us keep between the gulps of ghost, benders of erudition saying we're merely heaps of dashes and pieces of words. I say swords are needed, if the ruler is be our ward, if the Occupant is to be outward."

IN THE LOUNGE OF ATTRITION

Thrust of aerosol,

and a little snuff to loosen the wing.

Then some ointment before turning, miffed, toward the glint

as he kneeled down embarrassed, having spilt the silk so early in
the mimsy of his song:

"'Render unto Asunder what is Asudder's. Unto Grog what is
Grog's, but at least I got my vis-à-vis before my face
dismantled. Now with fat of child, sip of brandy, a bit of
poltergeist—
and the kiss-my-ass chronic pain of always swearing off the cream
curdles into one hell of a hallelujah. And hatched beneath
my skirt, a billow of milk
subsides from my wall, off some sleepy cliff until I'm swept into a
puddle,
where the knee whistles, prosthetics creak, and fully charred, I
give my regards

to the fist extending to darken the page, the withdrawal of the fist
the following hum."

Then a lull in the oval
surpassed

the pall of finally alone
appallingly fulfilled.

OBLATION

Half-hurled out the window, seemingly by my own hand, my arms were loaded with wood and I awoke beside the volcano but some vain hope of quelling the awful buzzing between where I was and where I was not assured me that the state of transition was clear and distinct in a note or drop of rain, although I'd never been fond of music, especially when flowing toward the bearer of the big cigar or the large pot of soup called proof.

That's when I was seized by Principal and beaten until I grew to love the ring or was it the success of success against the brute fact that I was in need of atonement for the hackneyed haecceities of ruin and confusion brought on myself by zipping and unzipping my rocket as if by coming apart by parting part I'd evade the invasion of adders.

But matter had become a matter no more private than cutting the skull out so I hocked my head to pure statistics, ducking out of only one lecture on the only snow recorded to offer my headmeat to intuition and quit my quibbling over distinctions between choice and selection

but what an asp I'd been all that talk about emptiness at the core what slithers off beat when all of history is a colon to nature only a little less than lustful, a little less than final having long since given up on applause, settling instead for ovation.

ORBIT

Ashes, aerosol, and a lull in the attrition

Where the light bends through the stalks and stalks the end
to a bluff of never exclusive, only miserly

a band of light, holy and irreparable, piano constantly pounding
almost noble almost burst

sets into remission an emanation
a pause in the halo or against some weighty Latin ending
the click and flick of instruments

or the ellipsis emphasized in completion
contradictory so immanent
a sensation of completion set loose
against the pulsars and parvenus of interruption
swooning through the lavish misuse of the word "white" as it is
        repeated in succession

to dust off the allusions
to plain sight or veiled estates

a lecture on heaven at zero degrees

ones and elevens, smudged ledgers
clot the excitation in the artery

then a lowering of the voice

narrowed to a squint or sliver, but still damp around the edge
pinioned to the capillary slightly abscessed
beneath the slowest gaze, emptiest glass

THREE ROCKS, THIRD DAY

Morning, gypped and cobbled
probes the glia and is restored to stillness
if stillness is through with moving through—
comes bold faced, bells on to suck a hard candy
moisten the flaps, gun-metal gray as dumb space
after whatever is covered and whatever can be
is subtracted from ashes, aerosol, and inattention
given the unwillingness to re-read, paid in loads of ink
or a reflex of ink, and leaking through the bag—asps
in the icebox, skinned assassins relax in the addition and
        are therefore omitted
as a matter of choice out of a lack of necessity
but each day the lump elects to stay close and go on

through the blaring lightness

of what is bright again, almost new

Jittery as a sine wave slouching through the sane room,
but here the slope is separate, tip of cup spilling the atoms, just a
      nip before noon
to diminish the emphasis on the delivery of possible emphasis
      placed on these jittery,
preoccupied morning where I awake to recite the ruler's name, and
      slur forth a drab wall
but if I stay on this side, if you by-pass the burn victim we just might
      glissade outside
to confront the petitioner standing bravely in the way of the sliding
      glass door
as it saws back and forth through the sirens rising
almost to the preferred level of exegesis where I control the curl
more like a jubilant pocket than a landscape just out of date
sliver of a finger still keeping the beat
one particle of ragtime, one rose plucked from success, and drawn
      directly from
the rusty valve of a night likely yet to prove eternal now that space
      does not occupy space buts stands at attention
almost ship-like, the wine-dark ruffle in the curtain, or against the
      curtain

THE OCCUPANT IN CONTEMPLATION

The bald one—
will turn out badly.

Too much talent colliding with ambition can't help
heading blearily toward fretful vacillation or any port in a swarm
    of siestas, especially when ruled vaguely with
splashy cheap editions,
all heap is lost

now that sun & moon are festooned in satellites, who will speak
    for the distractions, noise?
I've built a bullet of a universe insufficient to rivets or sense
full of seasonable beings who for any earth, any coast, any cost
will brave the gulf

for a lick at the dark clot or the rum of resurgence

but this one tosses my creatures about and pokes himself in the
    rib, oblivious to being abridged,
laments he's merely an outline of a blunt mass, former
light of my cigarette, watching the river for pep and depth so he
    can take leave
of the paper but takes takes takes the cake of persuasion,
though its footnotes make him squeamish

oh souvenir, oh suzerainty to come—
ignorant, the cause believes the sovereign is gone perhaps
awry, perchance to blurt—

but who's this standing here do

so that if I sneak ships before the moon
saying this one is a surrealist, this one a financier
does it make for a cabal of similarity if I take away sensation
for they are not evidence, certainly not "of sense"

they are form, even bent and waiting at the end of a ruler for end
       to the ruler
more percept than contemplation

simultaneously without objects, spokes
and still this dome stabs at wonder as if to stop or steel my
       perfectly lopsided wheel.

BLANK RESPONSE

Book under each arm, booze in the blood I trundle a trice
distracted but futile, though just this once I stroke past the
rusty sub and scurried out a ditch that ran off a rainy shoul-
der of another miniken I met behind the grogshop, most
oppressive, almost brassy as if a ray through two palms or
once more the tedious glower of the one who looks to be
looked at looking at me but the bit of time has passed, fleas
so whereas He was once fire-clad now seems surrounded if
gradually by ghosts, figments not of speech or quality but
duration whitening in length so as if one voice, even if Bool-
ean when in fact it was I who declined into incongruity, but
only in iteration, not truly taken to heart because it seems to
accrete at the middle even if debagged—its sticky like a knife
still extending still trailing off at the asterisk or the vibration
a little further down

the itch of imagination, dollop of jubilee rollicking against
precisely no example

but I knew now I was forever bent, though the mirror ball
passed through me—an outline of an egg in the fragments of
the mirror—

suddenly repaired to clarity by a clarity that was never there.

DEEP THROAT, DECLINED

When like palms the doors of the apothecary pry open—

my hand fumbles past the figs and poultry to pluck a passion fruit
color and shape of the most famous homeopath any white dress ever
      knew though so old it came apart before the eyes

all I remember is the sting of silver nitrate then swallowed up in
      cowboy boots with the hope of turning blue, but it was and
      was not you who passed
out in the grass a full three hours, more a question of address
if just to confirm the position of things, lest we are served another
      hilly-billy king whose
context has gone madly insufficient, not like
liberty or pride, but the ghost of them
breathing their echoes into our ovals,
caught in the throat, and beating more officious than
the continuous question of how long coming from the south or
how much jade on the trail home
when there is no girl with face of jade, no boy blue beneath
the heavens, blankets, heavens again
marshalling against that western light to greet the widow of the
      apparatus who waits at the end for an end to her wait
spreading like dementia across an otherwise
promising book everyone had found and put back, although once or
      twice hobbled back up—intoxicated—to tear it apart.

Followed instead the pithy comet that struck the helmet and swung
      out of bounds,
the moon in tow, so that it could not possibly be a question of
      coming together
or whether pleasure causes pleasure, but who's filling the script

if there be any difference that gives the slip.

OVER

Tapped out in a long hall

what careens out of the emptiness but disapproval or pleas
take the stairwell
it's only the terrible sound of ordinary language
singing through the exit wound
do not transfer into drowsiness
who do you work for that you are not so drowsy or well-versed in
        transferring out
how do you warble
and how may I eat the lily beneath your instructions when you
        have ghost on your breath and lisp a face?

My former employer, is it that participation precedes the value of
        work or does participation precede awareness
when it is all corrupt sky stiffening up beneath creases and pleats,
        creases
and pleats of ink and fusion

And yet there remains first rain, then intuition

they come and get us or is the abstraction all a form of drowsi-
        ness

I sleep in my boots and the days pass right over me, except for
        here and there
when I peak out the envelop, complicit
or fumble toward the pulse and perforation in the distance but
        farewell to the teal lows, carbonation at the cliff of a mirage
farewell to sorting us out, to *telos*
and farewell
to the caboose the color and shape of broth

unless the property of visibility could muster the weight to bring down at least the visibility of property, if its painstaking nonchalance wouldn't be overturned each spring like a capsule for an ache that was nothing much.

SUBLIMN

for EG *and* JD

Taking the pill to change the winds for, I was too soon on the horizon, though gunning for the moon when it veered off course, the same old splotch. Nightshirt deleted as I stretched out in that moonless closet, mirror smashed a thousand times but just two pulsars, their tails in my craw slung jointly into a *rond du jambe* where the comets scattered an ethereal light, as if a vast typographical mistake let the milk subside into some dumb lake. Now I was free to publish my mistakes, as if they were just heavy drafts, whistles in the knee, or prosthetic ovals leaking a certain dimensional perfection like dust Disallusionment or the dispersal of nothing final in the placenta of commas. Seeking occasion, I copped to the letter O and quickly succumbed to psychoanalysis

by purely etymological means, thus freeing myself from my more circular tendencies.

NOVA SUITE

Bright [1] at [2] last [3]
almost new

groping, trailing off

[1] First, you put on the white coat and a feeling that possibilities will arise. Punch-lines and hard-lipped paradox succumb to contradictory but corresponding coherence. Understanding may pierce a vague taste arising in a note of music: this correlates to the second, jarred state, a result of being stuck. The brute fact is some things are very similar in structure. Grain, sand, small twangy quakes between particles, the resin at the bottom of the super-colider of concern. Not a metaphysics, nor a discursive practice, but cooly extending through our boulders, a grid restates the grist and gist, indefinitely. Our affectations are blunted, but never our affection for the future.

[2] The smudge hovering in the doorway, then time to step around it, the glare of the glass sliding past.

[3] To leave the skin and enter the warm vernacular, to be very earnest, but never jarring. Simply urgent, entrenched, easily recited.

at last, a flash

as if almost off, then groping and out of breath
a breath breaking in a cramped loop

an antic wind or dropped ace spins through a black hole,

scratches the halo, nudges the ant
asphalt on the equator, tracks in the flour

then dark and bent,
absolutely still, almost infused

slightly flammable, a black hole sawed-off

then nothing, but a fugue in ordinary language

what is lived through taken apart by the lag between slack and
        description

the floor in intervals.

Cheap fuel, intervals[1] of powder, mildest silence

as if coming on strong or in plurals, strengthening without
      tradition.

A wormhole[2] comes on strong, tunneling the glint

the engine of glint
falsely meandering, strictly behavior

---

1 A ditch described as dark velvet seeks occasion. Some say it is the danger of
  seeing more stars than there are. Others fear the boards are as thick as a
  comma.
2 To leave the skin and enter the vernacular to be very earnest, but never
  jarring, simply urgent and entrenched, easily recited, slightly inflammable
  but brutal as event.

Still false, still bright, falsely still, a desultory pursuit.

The engine of glint[1] aced over and stabbing through

feathers drifting
white thread of white dress coming apart in the hand of those
      winged fellows lilting in

on dark furrows, and looped from the heat

won't come soon enough

thunderbolts won't steer things.

---

1 Later, the giant will ask his mechanic how it is that he knows the engine
won't start. The mechanic will give the answer, "Experience," but will leave
the giant somewhat unsatisfied, at which point the giant will seek a forced,
if unmotivated association between engines and eggs. For this reason, the
giant has never been extensive, only promiscuous.

Spindles, and rumors of angels, off but not filled in
lines and lines, all those pages striped in white
all those days lettering, all those ovals arriving in the same white
        dress,
only slightly more flammable than a white page striped
in white but folded in the foreground, and ruffling across the
        pure, immutable night
a terrace extended and mounting a trance
but just beginning its constant sweep
and across the terrace, a constant glint, then false, meandering
        pursuit

bores through, peeled off
the soft patter of carbon, oxygen

the necklace of smoke,
rings of ice

bleach in the foreground, a shift of weight

already a rink
of chores

seizures and decrees

always surrounded, always off

the scent of balloons, leaning

just getting started lets off

down a path up the start

the flick and click of implements

and drunken mergers
sodium across the axons

a nervous hum

a twang of summation, pang of summary at the tip of a cliff
terrace extending
lures the sodium across the axons
fizzles off at the tip

the tip of an eon bound to rest

the interleaving of ovals, bound balloons

compose a striation
in beginning gods, and from end to end, dark and bent
but always seeing double and slick with expectancy
touring the curve

a heave of cure

during a lecture on amnesia[1] given from a curb

1 A cramped state sometimes confused with diversity where entertainment
occurs in plain sight. The snow flake as footnote and the sky as aftermath of
foreign policy.

The upside curbs are in, smudged numbers
carbon on the hands, rubbed off

The hum and click of a strictly older testament

Heaven is without an old testament. This is heaven. One afraid
of patterns.

The pattern of one click and bleach across the mountains

Shifting their weight, always surrounded, almost off

Mountain evidence and a necklace of smoke.

A lecture of smoke.

Bright opposing sentences pinion and shift between rear views.

Lots and fixed forms, slow escalation. Then steam and ink across
the meltwash.

Ostensible fog, mostly places, sometimes song.

A grim moment of review, dim shimmer across a gray helmet of
      insomnia.

Sodium lights.

Mountain evidence and marginal revenge.

But, up and down high event all those days fizzling

A game of rangy light almost off almost through—
the arteries, thought left wavering—
between strict behavior and streaks on a bottle,
while in the valley, a shadow of an angel all morning over
the garage, the car running with the trunk clean,
the door coming down from the north.

But after the games of chance,
chance

what summates along the cilia
the sting of no one's exactly after you

while below
heat, light, and motion form a pageant.

Dizzy in the grass, a grassroots effort drifting blearily toward
brute fact

but the brute fact of the matter is that some things are very
similar in structure.

The interruption of screams, for example, did lead to the
buckling of the certain knees, but wingéd pursuit had long
since ensued.

A continuum of feathers drifting blearily in through holes in the
fence.

Trundling through the foreground.
Then bright at last.

As if an immense process of generalization had suddenly
become histrionic.

Only then, the smash.

Another shelf was restored each year, gaining a little more weight
like a limb.

Thus the pursuit of preening replaced the pursuit of preening
less.

Feathers fell before the eyes and so, at first, no one noticed that
the pasture had been tracked in at all.

At times, it behaved like a brand new field, sometimes a fairway.

Other times, a black wave crinkling through a cramped loop.

The valve of light

The tub in the sky where the giants wash their testicles

stood outside and stared over the terrace —
the stars where they are.

Already the sag of sky had loped through a very old window that
          finally acknowledged it never could sit still,
and so thickened at the bottom.

Always swollen.

The groundskeeper was imposing, all shoulders and immaculate like a ceiling.

Stood and walked toward the body opposite his, which was also unoccupied.[1]

The rest was scant and square, some pattern just slightly more recognizable than a straight line, but not as much of an imposition as an infinite number of points or a black eye.

As hope in posh medicine gave way to an excessive reverence for the cavalier. [2]

The key too big, the lock too small.

But who could not steal away on those nights when time plunged through empty sentences, and fell elegantly.

A chorus in the courtyard.

Another draft, another sought out occasion.[3]

The pasture appeared garish and overwrought, but never quite baroque.

---

1 A state like amnesia existing in posterity alone. In the male of the species, the memories of the man who was alive chiefly in his memory. A looped fugue.

2 White. What we love. Nothing covers the scent of jism on your fingers like armed conflict or sympathy for the working man. Think of him in winter, a stoic who cannot ski.

3 Between earth and ice but in no recognizable language: the solution. Like the solution to time and space, it lies in an artery outside space and time. Alone, therefore, unorganized. Elegant like silence is elegant so obsolete.

No matter how bright and new the field was,
still time to review. Always best to review.

It was, after all, my birthday and the first.

As it turned out, it was no private affair.

I received the news that the farm was kaput, and that I had all
    the hair I ever would.

Of course, I was breathless. In a hundred years, I'll be breathless
    still.

But never idle. Science says we'll have only begun knocking
    about.

Not you exactly and not me, but those first unconvinced atoms
    that will burst through that pure, unyielding
light, upend the shelving, scattering the documents—

—always swelling, always elevated, even at the bottom of the arc
    when that shiny black wrecking ball reels
into the core[1] emptiness—where all the wrecking balls are
    coming from anyway.

---

[1] The second law of thermodynamics decrees that the universe is drifting
inexorably toward "heat death" or a kind of universal blandness. But at least,
according to Glashow, no one can make the claim that this kind of research
is going to produce a practical device. Or as Paul once said, "Crime re-
quires funding."

Something perhaps passing the cheek.

[1]Out of the blastula
into the gesture
all texture, but no swing

bright as a decoy[2] structure of gas
entering the artery, star silt

a milting transmission, soot of

the day, stars fell

and gas inflated—

a black hole in the front matter

sodium light

but an infinite hyphen dismantled the face which was never
content simply to cover the head

1 The sky. To you, blue. To me, bereft of content. Rest between the roses and foreclosures as you would between worlds. Colors like consent arrest what you say of them. Speak only of conventions—between places and their winds. Green, for example, as colloquial as discontent. Time rent. A hushed shuffle.
2 According to ancient Mesopotamia, the circle deserved a healthy respect as a kind of divine bikini. It was not until Leo James Rainwater that the nucleus was believed shaped like a cigar, but individualism had long before been ignited.

that imperial whistle fizzled on—

another riveting song with no tune at all

the mummy of a music we had no more
except in briars along the shore and entangled in our hair
where the law of large numbers constantly nibbles

gas and grit[3]

gusting in like flu and rhetoric

[3] Particles have been accused of memory and monsters of leaving fossil records. But, all the laws of nature and the initial conditions themselves have conspired to make the carnival as compulsory as possible. Thus, the bread rises and the atom is detected. Later, the nose brushes the origin of the word democracy, though in fact it was not the result of having grown a face so much as exposing one. An over-achievement really, for the soul is still, painted still, like an axiom, but not a proper material so lacking composure.

pockmarks and paper doilies drift across

a perfect pitch

not just passing through what comes next as if we are satellites,
    but meatier

passing between the pitch

meteors, remarks

stars pitched and rising—pervasive as the edge or the flap

upside curbs in against what is over—
not the cap but the approach

a million miles excrete a phatic inch

then a pinched hit shafts the fanatic
bats rising through the synapse

nothing appears in the sham hollows but the embers of disjunc-
    tion

from one angle, the cigar of individuality,
from another a haecceity—the döppleganger of tedious nothing
controls the angle
of niceties

two cells disappear between whispers and metaphors of exchange

all pitch and no swing,
only texture attempts to quell the invoice

capital punishment or a shut out, but there remains
the dash mark
carved through the skull

two fronts collide in a flurry of receipts

dropping in like flu and rhetoric beneath the heap where all was
lost

a sexy-series of what-ifs dismantling the face[1]

pure unyielding light.

---

1 As a distant and approximate form of identity, the fossil permits resemblance
to subsist throughout all the deviations traversed by nature. This is why natural
history cannot be established as biology, for at this time "life" does not exist,
only beings that live. Later on, the world will become a lesson, but only for
monsters.

a terrace to a knot
not to return the hyphen
dividing the autotopsy into heaps and döpplegangers

bird irony bird.
autobiography[1]

a wave through an extravagant bell or a sentence trained in light

bright and opposite and brought on by the excessive use of the word
     "behavior"
to explain rings of ice
repetitious as an axiom
shelled sometimes
other times, a particle
in the verb just
as it
splits off

[1]   A horizontal line in space. A circumference ran past, each point entirely
coincident with each point along the horizontal line. They lived in an 180
degree arc until they fell out of love and were divided into two right angles.
The black void ate away at the white grid so that eventually they existed
solely as segments. Over time, each segment was superimposed on top of
other points by a philosopher who could prove the existence of this infinite
abundance of horizontal lines, but had no confidence in it. "All of a sud-
den, there was nothing but me."

to circle the atoms of a lost identity or to clot the artery behaving
    like a savior in the pure
    unyielding anonymity[1]

of taking flight and colliding.

at the edge, privilege dots a dead thing, soot
makes its gains in the blanks, falls
and burns through its shadows across the tenth of a dollar
a series of zeroes enters the blood
iron exchanged with bones of lead
a permanent dispute enlarged with paper
embroidered across the gesture
nine parts scratched out, a relation
one part fraudulent noise remains in a relation
to a particle fluttering in the placenta
the ominous clicking of adjacent rooms
distant articulation never together always trudging
vehement as attrition and provoking the worm
against the long arm of the lawn

a hole of authority lifted from a leitmotif[2]

---

1 An electron is identical with every other electron, but leaves falling are not
  leaflets dropped by bombers. No theory is a sincere alternative to war. No
  jaguar circles a territory quite like an orbit. Taking off your clothes is not a
  revolution.

2 Bohr, in a series of speeches in Copenhagen late 1920s, held that subatomic
  entities such as electrons have no real existence; they exist in a problematic
  limbo of many possible superposed states until forced into a single state by
  the act of observation. The cosmos, Wheeler said, is a participatory phe-
  nomenon requiring observation. Solid states, like fugues, are a fool's purga-
  tory.

Broken parrot warps north.

True north is gathering force.

Silence careening through us.

No rocks to roll back, but many ways to leave the room.

One is humiliation. Another carnal love.

One a black hole, the other a pronoun.

Whether to break off the skin or merely go dry from the heat of
red ibises flapping in the sheets.

Bats rising from beneath the bridge, at the foot of night, in the
dark game of rain not falling.

A warm vernacular.

Accommodated by discipline.

The perfume of resistance mounts a lousy waltz against the tool-
making talents.

Slips egregiously toward the window of devotion.

But the widow of the apparatus waits at the end for an end to the
wait

A point is reached, comes to a point—slants, shuts— then the
        shape of a pear [1] gradually dissipating

a void between the letters and details of the window appearing to
        come to a point.

A matter of re-entry like the moat or a vocation as solid as steel
        wool or blue thread of blue imported sky

that comes apart in the hurricane between space and form

boots then confidence

to steer through the pragmatic archipelago

as if a moral necessity or a shameless nebulosity bends the ruler
        as sight is bent and the body vacates—

light arcing through a tower [2] set in reverse
vibrations and guesswork but the time has come

for a joke told backward and lobbed against a screen of despair

1 The General claimed to reach it, but to use it without mastery was a ques-
   tion for the Grounds Keeper to whom the pear merely occurred, another
   irreducible impropriety.
2 The tower retracting here is a reference to "mere rebels" and useless love.
   There was, in fact, never any single monument, but there were rainbows
   and pronouns. A kind of cosmic foam that fizzles up on the rim.

pulling back through the fronds—

                          one tenacious cave

almost signs of transcendence, shafts of a phatic if transitional
        species but absurdly current with unlimited surcease
brings on another surd in the maze of experiment
troops in a loop born in a current

the time has come—

come to a point warped up in epiphany and reached at last through
        vibrations and guesswork.

Filing in decimals   whistling ovals
          laminating descants   demoting towers

the moats splashes out of its vacancy

a vacant necklace flares every half-hour

while molecules shower secants

the toll is carried like a loaf of bread

the bread arrives in the shape of a head

as sure as the skin or double knot in the shoulders

as they collide against the skylight

syllables whistle
decimals escalate
refuse to be patient or have anything to do with still or silt
on sideways afternoons in a vacant republic while letters float
      through the slit[1] in the crown[2] but end at concrete and
      crickets
as they collide in the cortex
where an alphabet begs to go on

---

1 The many ways to leave a room seem less urgent than whether to break the
   skin off and merely go dry from the heat. Faced with such a dilemma, why
   all this flap about red ibises turning up illegally, wondered the greenskeeper.
2 The other revolutions had better hats.

a detachment of skin,
mock curtain, mock rain
a reproduction detached from motion
is not raining or instantaneous or clouded by the guesswork
vibrating the tonic, and poured in tenths
it's dangling so not finished
like a neutral road tangled in the moss of the soma
burning in the neurons of our ethics,
an army of nerves not at all optimistic

just as they slip the bit,
      bits

or a loop of lips moving the mouth in patterns

through the knock of device and assemblage,

a drone not in mind, but in a ruffling leaf or man shivering
midway through a puff of smoke a cigar,

count cigarettes watch the river

snow, and the mind galloping

tuft of cloud, not stars of disjunction, just night

extending its jar, sawing through the brain of a jaguar,[1]

tapping his foot in dispute

---

1 Icons sought in circumferences, fluctuations in banality, bright at last.

snow fell with no style

asterisks grew robust

but everything went white and conjoined

a moony rain but at once, both

gun metal gray

the way music or copper on the tongue spreads to the throat

Clouds the color of smoke,
leaves rustling,
cows shifting,
the crow,[1] the count
a thin rainy thinning
in a lecture on carrying on
no tin in the pocket, no ashes of access
just risen fragments, continued brilliance
falling after the lash
thin as a feather against half-life of an archive
withdrawing from the next line
while observing the breath
ashes never at rest

---

1 According to the crows, one crow could destroy all of heaven, and accord-
ing to the General, heaven is immune because it signifies precisely the im-
possibility of crows. The Grounds Keeper maintains both are correct. The
impossibility of paraphrase seems to potentiate the complaint. Each attempt
to start in the other, though similar, direction reinforced the unattainable
reality of mastery: its apparent failure comes very close to love, a common
love, where "art" is free to be a verb again.

Cloud tangible, stars that wobble.

But not raining.

Ashes convoy toward the floor in intervals
the only cargo, a dead moan
or an axon eroding
but the infinite was not a problem of atoms as tiny universes
but of science[1] as a vibration

entropy as appropriation of work, boards, planks

leaks, widths

a tenth of an asteroid used for an asterisk

always a chink in the infinite regress
effacing the rose or a coat of foam
metallurgic as memory—

where birds are best—

                              set aside

---

1 "I'd rather be a professor in Basel, than a retired god," says the General over
   the pings of the pinball machine. The geisha turns and coughs, but the
   undergraduate persists, "Do you like money? If so, I have no flaws."

A myelin froth: the neurons pivot and the feathers are cast

squandered footsteps, acoustic discretion

the hero's salt and the hard water
cast an electrical gesture

sparrows expressed in sorrow reduced to a copious needle,
atomic suds
swerving around the hive of the ghost
trickled against the stalk of the purpose

    a squall of lint embroidered across low light

chips away corrupt sky and it looks like rain may not be
      needed

here the bees beat juicy shadows around the nose of the
      giant

an abrupt luster gums up the knees of gardener

a corrosive music sags across the window, and fraying at the
tip of the tongue

blue ceiling [1] drowning in the blue rug [2]

spreading like brass on the tongue of the General

---

1 Attraction abstracted by abstraction.
2 Abstraction distracted by abstraction.

while the rug of the ocean spreads across the ridges of the forest

the glass around the forest and the jaguar pacing along the
    shoulder

as a quark bounces through a white satchel, a cloud withdraws,

the jaguar throws one ankle outside the jar[1] of death[2]

the sound of paint stamped across a receipt

yields a slick yes   yellowing in a jar[3]

---

1 Sensation as opposed to sense. Reference here to Francis Bacon both to his
brush strokes and to his aphorisms which were an attempt, he claims in
later interview, at painting directly on to the nerve ending. A philosopher of
the same name, unfortunately, worked elsewhere to remove space between
what the painter would later capture as triptychs: the impossibility of giants
and generals in the same room, much less the same man.
2 Abstraction abstracted by abstraction.
3 Even a drop of water falling lightly upon a rock will eventually bore a hole.
Like all watering holes, this is the origin of treaties and disputes.

a glitch in a loop of nights knocks the technician into sleep

a sleek system shimmies down a rope

barbed wire is wrapped around a doll

numbers, powders, creases and pleats erased in foam and kept
     requests

the shadow of the desperado quivers in the reeds and never quite
     finishes

jaguars turns up along the shore of a postcard
or a bag is boiled or the night is scratched by a grain of rice

ink oozes from the inside of an egg

the scent of a balloon absorbs a comfortable room

corpses form syllables that go yellow a syllable at a time
and a bruised ankle stirs a blue river

the river of never, a bruise of information
as in the word "slender" not quite at tip of the tongue

but one comes back to it when the solar panels fall
or the shadow of the desperado quivers in the reeds and never
     quite finishes
again as another northerner rises and is repelled

their shrill imprint etched in the gasworks

The northern syllable of water

cold

bereft

the heir[1] of transparency

proprietor of vibrations

the impact of guesswork

arriving after the illness

by way of circumlocution, the temperature of a comfortable
     room

is dismembered by the numbers and tempered by a draft

or an antic wind that twists along the path of foam

or composed of snow under the skin, the temper of decimals

an escalation of content

collides against thrown signs and same things

---

1 In an earlier version, the nothing himself beheld the nothing that is not
there as well as the nothing that is, but here wind across grass and good
government have the same fate as the edge of sea or a drafty mind: blue
wrongs green. The parrot swallows its screech. December delivers the both
ways of January. All futurisms strictly anachronism.

but its smoke where there is smoke and there is parlance where
    the ceiling is streaky

the floor exaggerated, even in intervals

a drop of foam[1]
or dollop of force
the dribble of irrefutable error
desolate as a monad in a comfortable room
when the craft warning is a kind of brown tweed
misread from a book that was carefully crafted after the
        patter of nomads
brown tweed all day split belly of a fish
and no Buddha
but every bit as dusty as the ruins of confusion
a loop of ovals or the illegibility of an oval

an insulation

smoke pushing across the darkest shore
maybe solid
impunity as an insulated current
a second chance where one word is still enough

an insult that stays the crowd
an infiltration of pulses or perforations
a stark syllable between the cilia
a quark filtering through the fold
an angel found hanging from a pulley

---

1 Our lather who is in curved and thick space, hollow is the sequential advance echoing through your name.

stark and furiously unaccompanied, but adequately ruled if
     negatively charged
static pulled from my pocket[1]

---

1 It is well known that besides the errors common to the tribe, there is within each of us his or her own private cavern or den and that within this cavern there is a tribe burrowing below the jungle looking for the idols of the cave and finally, quite sore, they reach the southern core of the earth. It is here, far from the chill in our bones, that we are most pale and therefore in no danger of cannibals. The fugue is master and what is unreached is shelved.

Pouch of decoys, ache o'clock
the loam of phantoms, the clink of coins

"I stack and
you lift. You lift,
and I stack."

Not so hard in this pure unyielding closet
where the moon is bent
gravity [1] knocking like a giant
the gist and grit of rocks that find their way into the eye

like clouds but not raining
only ruffling the sky [2]

[1] Neither dark ships, nor sea gulls, not even the carpeting can escape what is
not separate in a qualitative sense at all. Neither can it be said, strictly speak-
ing, that a body that is dropped has a speed—no matter how fast it falls;
rather it has a "infinitely decreasing slowness" like nights, oceans, and im-
mortality. All are a qualitative movement within the *nomus*. It is true that
routes, paths, global waves are set out like school clothes the night before.
However, none of these can keep the dark automobile from reaching a con-
stant relation with the littoral. Hence it is said: Night, ocean, immortality
posses the same fortune as the giant and the groundskeeper. Each contains
an infinitely decreasing amount of anonymity. Thus all are associated with
nomads, noumena, and any other points of view unknowable from history.
Still, we are not talking about a state of nature nor are we speaking of a
science of routes, paths, and global waves. We are speaking only of organi-
zation, its impossibility of being mastered. That is to say, love.

[2] Diversity. Sometimes referred to as reading room. What is never reread un-
ravels here in the blue thread of blue habit.

a knot
not confidence
an ablation of confidence
via secret ballots and the constant terrace
despite light turnouts and forgetting
a fugue state where figuration is saturated
        and not a big dark carpet
but a satellite of blue becoming a habit[1]
of sight

while, we, like satellites
orbit the other side of the broom
a kind of vindication against science,

and its secret, immutable ballet.

---

1 Not indifferent. Sadly lyrical. The sort of lyricism that results directly from
an apprehension of events in their extremities. For example, the fact that
universe is enormous and superficial, and yet, due to a melancholy ten-
dency, it manages to appear only during one part of the day and in a way
swords and secret ballots can't quite capture..

The carpet is covered
with a map of the carpet.

Yards and yards of why
would you ever
go out again[1]

from this room
or little moon
moving north
you and you and you[2]
wanted to be a mountain
"art" wanted to be a verb again
but "I stack, you lift and you lift and I stack"

the floor plan leaves off.

A habit of sky, gist, and grit.

1 Yielding and not yielding, wind across grass, breaths and hesitations.
   Monday rules the week, but is sure to be surpassed. By nature if not privi-
   lege.
2 A pronoun may exceed the invention of sense just as natural history leads us
   to believe that the enemy is winged. And any love is possible.

Sacked by rumors, limber as a fragment
hunkered beneath a shell—

an edge to come, and the terrace waiting
the fugue-state where figuration is saturated
watching the alternative[1] for a rumor
come to nothing but an egg
that is red
beneath the fringes
of this mountain[2] on the edge of the terrace
where the skin detaches
a mock skin, mock curtain
evidence that no egg floats[3] over the body,
just lint and flinty consequence
slithering off beat
toward the decoy
in the creases and folds

of a pocket.

1 Sometimes referred to as single-mindedness.
2 A shoulder.
3 The parakeet reaches the *polis*. The pole is not there. The tree edited, the
mouth moving in patterns. Why not keep yours shut and see how the room
looks then. A curtain maybe later. But for now, an hour with your arm in
the wall. In this fashion, the *polis* is forgotten like a knife trick. Death man-
ages to go on, but only as a language of statement. Give up that nonsense
about mountains.

The sky is a convoy

spitting out the little pill

soil in my pocket

slowly washed mountains, rocks
that begin like a beak begins
and end like a cavity that moves from tooth to tooth
with a wrecking ball above
and below a din in the mission
the domination of motion
the fugue headlong
so relational [1]

but a ship there is lonely

the loneliness of astronauts
who won't stick to ship but stack and lift

beneath a nebula,

thickening
but won't rain

1 Like the soul, an exhalation, but not of the individual body. Of the mob.

the furnace churns out clouds and convoys,
particles of friction cause a track in the music
to collude with the cracks through a corrupt ride
a scratched out future where gumption won't assail structure
but a series of facts in the shape of paragraphs

gist and grit go knocking about

while one electron
attracts a rock to and from a self-discovery
but is missing until sought by
a hole that wobbles
like a word of light
outside the pure glass jar of death
used in the elision
an indifference to the depiction of the moon
as an immense talk
where an egg accepts its paradox as an outline of a rock
the shell of an egg[1]
in the rear view, on a pointed roof[2]
inert

---

1 The egg warbled, grew immanent, surrounds. A baroque pearl or slouch
toward an infinity of finite slumps. How the pearl is, is outside the pearl.
Potentiality rises from beneath the egg and surrounds it as a halo or shell,
but only after the pearl is able to act. What changes are not things, but their
calibrations. Sameness, thrown signs, and a matter of degrees are all de-
ployed to establish that the one brick is still in place.

2 "But these black holes I call pronouns are but a blue thread against a peda-
gogy of ceilings." —the Grounds Keeper.

Saturns[1] or Plymouths[2] are inert.

Rocks in the eye,
work

the sky is filled with rocks
and work

the work of a species
or a cult
brought by Mars rock
or placed in pocket
like a ring
so as not to collide
with the first offer
or divide the intellect
but is inert
insects collide against the skylight

against the work of a species,
the rock won't roll back or
sound alike and is cavalier
therefore inert[3]

---

1 Because some infinities are larger than others, the supply of demand at times surpasses the demand for a supply. At such points, the idols of the marketplace and idols of the theater overlap. The cavalier is but one example and is not suitable for traversing the cave.

2 The success of success seemed to depend on it and on the helping, friendly manuscript dropping in like flu. Only after the act.

3 This angered the beehive into jive-ass ideas about bilingual syllogisms and equal charges between molecules. Every electron is interchangeable with every other so no distinction was being made between echoes and decibels not even by the imperial whistle who felt the whole matter was as obvious as the face of death or as immaculate as a dish of milk.

The bulk of bunk intuits the limbic brain.

Sheer flux

grows more sawed-off

the planet needs signs of ink

hormones tunnel, worms grow comfortable with words
and the space careening through the hippocampus
drains white as a dish of milk
or dissolves like a forest
rumored to dissolve on
the tongue

but is calibrated when not suggested

by meters or guesswork
bent from beneath
by the dent of revision

left in a halo

along the region of event.

region is a rivet[1] with voltage
from the ship that won't be but vibrant
like a toss

a particle between a perforation

a previous indiscretion
maintained by not raining
through resemblance a punctured aspiration
passes into subtraction
to subtract the stillness
that refers to the previous passage
about returning to the spasm

so hard to revert, it must fail,
so hard to fail—one does—

1 The exact value of any puncture is determined not by supply or demand,
but by whether or not the lords of attrition are willing to acknowledge their
mission.

—one does succumb to the still life of a levitation

to a cup of rum

the geese return and the guess

reasserts
the red splotch on a nightshirt

but the guest of a thing
is the effect it had—

viciously emptied

and steeped in reference

a reverence densest in the slur of discrepancy

of staying close and coming to rest as it is due
while meaning anything if there be anything between
the "and" and "again"

besides resilience and guesswork

an equation won't.[1]
but a[2] pocket will,
yes a pocket will like an eclipse in the forebrain

an aspirin in parenthesis
the aftermath of ellipsis
moon looming over rent promised
or the destruction of California
long overdue like relatives and residuals
but smart as a stripe, ripe as a neuron
hedged between sins and naps
third rate symbols—of "the one brick still in place"
says the old man dreaming of another drink
no pupils, no particle of light
print out of nothing
dying *causa sui* in a line of nights,
preoccupied with the taxis that take him apart

---

1 The grass eventually devastates the greenskeeper. The nature of attraction
is that a walk in the woods will never do by which is meant this mountain
does not concern, has not occurred, is not through. Or everything is more
beautiful in disuse.

2 Reach an entrance. Structure of a gas entering a block, algae ambushing
the sundial. The figure appeared, passed through a fog, bent over, inhaled a
stone and mistook it for a mood. The idols of cave kicked in his teeth. It was
a chance to win or arrive or successfully be embarrassed.

vicious contortion
ignition of wind, grit,
inch of day
verb in the corners
in need of something to do
for one cold syllable
or one trip to the moon
even for a hug in the future
anything instead of lifting furniture no lighter
than one bloodred giant
in a dark ship
clouds tangible
ripping through the clickergame
of "I stack and you lift."

You lift and I stack.

Heavy as the hackwork of a hole[1] in the fence[2]
an interval of ovals and indentions in the grass
left by poised testicles and chiming through a bright opposite
     sentence
pinioned yearning and endless re-posing of law[3]
that leaves its last, lewd rose —
composed of minimums and iridium
in another molecule gone sideways,
traced over and secluded
a moebius of days and nights
senseless as this pure, unyielding light

1 Silence careening is an event not to be confused with the lending of lungs
or attrition. Rather, fluency is the result of no one being after you.
2 Fences are curiously associated with idols of the tribe and not of the market-
place. All fluency is a matter of duration and not quality. In the right light,
barbed wire sparkle like the heavens.
3 The crown was useful, even preventative, but empty as a slight space or
narrow chance. Sunlight, stays there, rustling. Two by two. To the trees.
Taking leaves often tears apart, the called off lark: what a convention is
consent. Dark tomorrow, dark hereafter. A sliver of silver in the clever talk
of pain. Accepting the first offer but avoiding the ring. It drills a glint through
the head. As if more air was more success, but without the hope of death,
for the victim's alive. And trees do what the wind asks. The crows have
cracked. Everyone accepts what an appliance is the bird.

entirely quaffed, often truant
then a little at a time
the shadow of what is done if doing what you read
and not reading what you do
in the name of what you like or in a matter of how do you do
but in parallel to the severing of the spine or the number of turns
     in a kiss
when the words return, entirely relaxed
and meeting in the dimness of a rink of chores
the holes in words are a set of instructions
leading to a detonation —
the raw force of a cough that lends its dampness to the hand
the tip of the finger tapping up a crumb and cavorting with the
     fact this comment got nothing to do with you or
the sag in the glass from the heat of a detonation
the hotel[1] detonating last night in a city moving back and forth

---

1 Commonly associated with ghosts, but more precisely associated with births
and conceptions, as in the case of Holderlin who spoke of death becoming
apparent only in children — "the soul of their parents' acts." Lucretius, as
well, warned us that the seed was gathered from the whole body. Given the
fact that a part could not be infinitely divisible, for this would imply that is
was also infinitely large. Thus, the conception of absence was created where
saturation would do. For example, the whole of a hotel contains a hole
which is not separation or death, but an atomic language, according to
Epicurus. Aristotle was not satisfied: no one could explain the cause of mo-
tion. The groundskeeper suggested that motion was merely an attribute of
matter which like language, death, and particle physics extended through
everything. In other words, artificiality occurred through natural processes.

through the risen fragments and driven conclusions
where the *nomus* accretes a pasture and roses pose
just off the fold of another dimension—
derivation of boulders, cliffs with scrag grass drying
of facts flat but bent by gravity, cut loose
from purpose and reeling through paragraphs
or for our purpose,

success[1] and failure[2]

---

1 Because it is a result of all the atoms (of which the philosophers were formed) now gathering once more in our breath and yet we are just as conscious as when the Cartheginians were attacking on all sides. No discomfort endures, only its extension or the name of its extension.
2 Mind, used here, as a hotel rather than a simple sensation is most often depicted as a hole where hostile joy chokes off any cellular transmission. Hence, abstraction is the preferred locale.

If, however, probability[1] is a version of aversion
plus and minus the blinking parts

If certain appropriation cannot be made
in gallant verses irredeemably furrowed
where streaks and stripes are palmed off

or troops were reduced to tropes [2]

Then probably this is why gambling [3] is exciting.

---

1 Ambience
2 In order to avoid confusion with statements made by certain curators, the author must be explicit that the relationship here is not that of river to rivet, but once again to the Monk who said "Simple ain't easy."
3 Consider the two statements: "There's an adder in your backyard" and "There's a lawn in your backyard." Certainly, the first is more rare (especially if correct) and the second quite plain (even if uncommon). However, the law of large numbers would suggest that both are equally meaningful. On the other hand, the presence of the adder suggests a privileging of the middle ground. So the oval is gradually surrounded by ghosts, fluctuations.

A matter of cadence in the manner of measure—

Transmissions summarized in wire, struck down in frills, day and
day sawed-off

Still, a kind of stamina—icons in the circumference

Attenuation of lesions accumulated in addenda

Tail of a lizard, tip of an eon branching off through a blizzard of
religions saluted in leisure
and refuted by
how surely others have done it, but that's about all,

yes, that'll be all.

Unto Asunder's what is Asunder's.

Unto Grog, Grog's.

                        The sand reduced to glass.

A hall of mirrors structured like a gas

Slow and aristocratic so all in one piece

A single mirror hides anything,
but two mirrors to demean the topic.

What remains are mere demons, daubed in nothingness,
   conducive of nothing, become one long comet
or an air pocket, drifting into the glass.

Glass gradually reduced to sand.

An opaque future reflex, reflected in Immanence.

Recited and brushed past like a little death or a simple matter of
   documents changing hands
by way of a stroke or spurt of paint that clings forever to the
   bright, uniform of fact, gradually reduced.

An exsanguination of demons —

To destroy clarity with clarity [1]

To get to the matter that remains —

An oval in stone.

A slab of pond.

Allpox. Education.

---

[1] On this point, the Faculty of Theology contradicts the greenskeeper and thus the ancient appeal to the articles of Paris (who has gone a long time without seeing beauty). In place of the greenskeeper, a philosopher was sent, heavily robed and wearing his bat-winged hat, but lacking any formal understanding of the arteries. He returned to describe a dream in which he had performed his own autopsy in the hope that the story would prove useful to those who were awake.

The stars continue nothing, I continue them
from beneath these fobbed off robes

despite the blow to the head

this top keeps revolving

around whatever is not appropriated

by a blow to the head, by a slab of stone.

Above, demons orbit,
beneath all that remains
bastions of access rarely accessible
even through experiment or another blow to the head.

Their commotion a kind of loneliness, a common luster.

At first just a fibrillation.[1]
Then the knocking.

The demons' comet.

A puddle of red.

---

1 Not a conception of time wasted, but an event in the extreme. A drone of
the imagination.

Drink one and you shall see —milk is pavement.[1]

It pins you down as stars go out.

Pinpoints[2] in the sky are limousines slinking.

To distrust them is simply to imitate
at a gradually reduced speed.

And reduced to the point where all one listens for is the music

spin.

---

1 Crossword.
2 Cloudbursts.

Satellites and limousines spin beneath the curbs in the claims
Tops crash to the floor.

Revolving [1] tops are not limousines.

They are the possessions [2] of children [3] who receive them
once a year
at a festival where horns [4] commemorate intricate tissues,
        intervals of mild powder, occasional floor.

Above the table, drones of abstraction [5] impersonate the dead.

---

1 Ovalness.
2 If upon licking the forehead of a child, you perceive a salt taste, this is cer-
   tain proof that he or she has been fascinated. To remove the spell, apply
   bacon. In the case of extreme fascination, only fat of jaguar will suffice.
3 At this age, Bourdieu says, each is a little bourgeois.
4 Funnel-shaped.
5 Pudgy boys. Also believed to be the reason we have mermaids. Sometimes
   equated with poetry.

The room with the revolving top erodes into tables and chairs.

A lowering of the voice to a sword. Hovering of a sword over a
cake.

An oval rises, bare breasted in a way that rivals music, and flops
out around the table
her tail a scabbed, but talented prosthetic—

Limousines are hostile cake, she says.

Turns, coughs, and then faces the lens,[1]
To hell with these horns, she says, *I am looking for the one with
talons.*

She swallows the slab mistaken for a mood.

Whatever hovers is the sun.

---

1 On this detail, both audience and author agree to defer to a certain optom-
etrist, who despite his fluency in Latin and alleged cruelty to spiders, man-
aged to define the imagination as thus: the world plus the idea of an inter-
nal cause. Love, he wrote in his treatise on ethics, is obviously pleasure plus
the idea of an external cause. On the question of whether or not this implies
that he was an adder, the two sides are splayed.

I am looking for a star that creams me.

Inside the limousine, it is light and dark.

Smoke from the tail pipe and dints in fancy metal.

Here she learns there are no such thing as talons.

There are only limousines, scrimmaged statements and
  panels along the shore.

In the morning, a slight tunnel or a slurred routine.

In the evening, missing winks.

Night brings on the law of falling bodies.[1]

At the core, doors

unproven clicks in corridor

a roll of nickels tightening in a fist.

---

1 Always homely if not hospitable.

Who blurts [1].

---

1 One must not accept the aesthetic of the bomb if one hopes to call attention
   to its evil. For example, what ordinary language fails to appropriate from
   duty, fate, and other durable accidents. On this point, the texts of the peti-
   tioners, curators, and groundskeepers are identical: "I regret that I have but
   three billion lives to give for my country." Dates vary. A point made by the
   giant: stress on those days was placed on the parahuman aspect of the or-
   gies.

There are no such thing as talons, she explains, *There are only limousines.*

She heads into the sun swearing she can handle it. *Statements don't change things.*

He says, *I have not one bathing suit. It's a matter of principle.*

Palms bend, the beach heaves.

This is not the ocean, she says, *this is only blue. The sky has beached in the air. The air is cluttered with fins and the tropic[1] is dropping. But I must go in. I've come without any skin.*

---

1 When the adders take the void for purpose, and the void take the purpose as a kind of avoidance, dolphins no matter how deep grow nervous, having endured only through accident. Accidents, like porpoises, should not be confused with liberty, for example, buying the farm. Nevertheless, it cannot be avoided: back at the fort, folks are counting on us.

NEW AMERICAN POETRY SERIES (NAP)

30. *New and Selected Poems,* Charles North
31. *Polyverse,* Lee Ann Brown
[WINNER NEW AMERICAN POETRY SERIES COMPETITION 1996]
33. *The Little Door Slides Back,* Jeff Clark
[WINNER NATIONAL POETRY SERIES 1996]
34. *Tales of Murasaki and Other Poems,* Martine Bellen
[WINNER NATIONAL POETRY SERIES 1997]
35. *Atmosphere Conditions,* Ed Roberson
[WINNER NATIONAL POETRY SERIES 1998]
36. *Nova,* Standard Schaefer
[WINNER NATIONAL POETRY SERIES 1999]

For a complete list of our poetry publications

write us at Sun & Moon Press
6026 Wilshire Boulevard
Los Angeles, California 90036

SUN & MOON PUBLICATIONS
OF THE NATIONAL POETRY SERIES

1994 / Pam Rehm *To Give It Up*
[selected by Barbara Guest]
1995 / Juliana Spahr *Response*
[selected by Lyn Hejinian]
1996 / Jeff Clark *The Little Door Slides Back*
[selected by Ray DiPalma]
1997 / Martine Bellen *Tales of Murasaki and Other Poems*
[selected by Rosmarie Waldrop]
1998 / Ed Roberson *Atmosphere Conditions*
[selected by Nathaniel Mackey]
1999 / Standard Schaefer *Nova*
[selected by Nick Piombino]